ANIMAL KINGDOM
SNAKES

Written by
Rebecca Phillips-Bartlett

Genius Kid

North Star
KIDS

Snakes © 2024 BookLife Publishing
This edition is published by arrangement with BookLife Publishing

sales@northstareditions.com l 888-417-0195

Library of Congress Control Number:
2024952949

ISBN
978-1-952455-33-9 (library bound)
978-1-952455-89-6 (paperback)
978-1-952455-70-4 (epub)
978-1-952455-53-7 (hosted ebook)

Printed in the United States of America
Mankato, MN
092025

Written by:
Rebecca Phillips-Bartlett

Edited by:
Elise Carraway

Designed by:
Ker Ker Lee

All facts, statistics, web addresses and URLs in this book were verified as valid and accurate at time of writing. No responsibility for any changes to external websites or references can be accepted by either the author or publisher.

Photo Credits — Images courtesy of Shutterstock.com, unless otherwise stated.

Cover — cellistka, PetlinDmitry, Alvydas Kucas, Rosa Jay, Eric Isselee, Aastels, Chase D'animulls, DSlight_photography. 2—3 — blackboard1965, RMMPPhotography. 4—5 — chrisbrignell, Dr Morley Read, Kurit afshen, Chase D'animulls. 6—7 — Eric Isselee, Sam Ives. 8—9 — GoodFocused, Mark_Kostich, Eric Isselee, fivespots. 10—11 — Milan Zygmunt, Eric Isselee, Matt Jeppson. 12—13 — Rusty Dodson, fivespots, Kurit afshen, Padodo. 14—15 — Joe McDonald, Photosite, Suham Chakraborty, muhamad mizan bin ngateni. 16—17 — ShutterStockies, Stuart Hamilton, off5173, Creeping Things. 18—19 — Michiel de Wit, Lester Graham. 20—21 — Kurit afshen, Andrea DiSavino, GoodFocused, Stephane Bidouze. 22—23 — Sklo Studio, cynoclub, Eric Isselee, Kurit afshen, ermess.

CONTENTS

Words that look like this can be found in the glossary on page 24.

SNAKES

Close your eyes and imagine a snake.
What do you see?

Perhaps you see a huge anaconda.
Maybe you imagine a small, striped
ribbon snake. There are some things all
snakes have in common.

Snakes are reptiles. Reptiles are dry, scaly animals with backbones. Reptiles are cold-blooded. Their body <u>temperature</u> is controlled by their surroundings.

Unlike most reptiles, snakes do not have arms or legs.

DID YOU KNOW?

An animal with a backbone is called a vertebrate.

BODY OF A SNAKE

From cobras to corn snakes, all adult snakes have these main body parts:

SCALES

A snake's body is covered by colorful, shiny, or smooth scales. Scales are like hard layers of skin.

BENDY BACKBONE

Snakes have bendy backbones. They can slither around by moving their bodies into different shapes.

FORKED TONGUE

All snakes have tongues that are split at the end. This is called a forked tongue. Snakes use their tongues to smell. Forked tongues help snakes find where a smell is coming from.

NO EYELIDS

Snakes do not blink. Their eyes are protected by a layer of clear scales.

TYPES OF SNAKES

There are more than 3,500 different types of snakes.

Some snakes are venomous. Venomous snakes carry <u>venom</u> in their heads. They pass this venom on with a deadly bite.

Venomous snake fangs

The most venomous snake in the world is called the inland taipan. Its bite can even kill humans.

King cobras are venomous snakes. They are known for their hood-like flaps. They spread these flaps out when they feel scared.

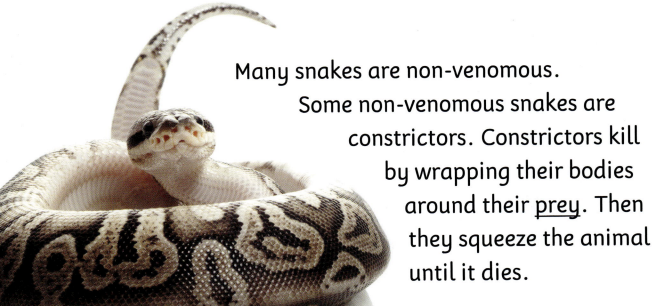

Many snakes are non-venomous. Some non-venomous snakes are constrictors. Constrictors kill by wrapping their bodies around their <u>prey</u>. Then they squeeze the animal until it dies.

HABITATS

A habitat is a plant or animal's natural home. A habitat has everything a plant or animal needs to live, including food, water, and shelter. Snakes live almost all over the world.

Hundreds of different snakes live in the Amazon rainforest.

Lots of snakes make their homes on the ground. Western ground snakes live in North America. Their scales can be different colors and patterns.

Saharan horned vipers live in sandy deserts.

11

AMAZING SNAKE ABILITIES

Snakes have lots of <u>adaptations</u> that help them cope with difficult habitats.

COLORFUL CREATURES

Snakes come in many different colors. Some snakes match the color of their surroundings. This helps them hide themselves. Other snakes use bright colors to warn animals that they are dangerous.

EEL THE HEAT

Most snakes do not have good eyesight. Instead, they have holes in front of their eyes that feel heat. They can feel heat when warm-blooded prey is nearby.

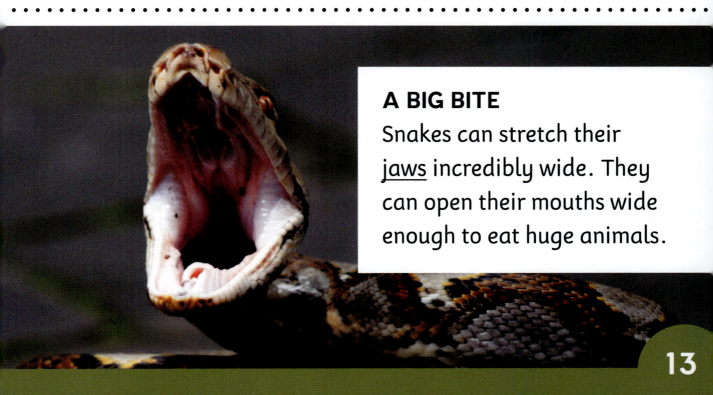

A BIG BITE

Snakes can stretch their jaws incredibly wide. They can open their mouths wide enough to eat huge animals.

HELPFUL SNAKES

Snakes help humans and the planet in many ways.

MEDICAL MARVELS

Some snake venom can be deadly. However, scientists have come up with ways to use snake venom in medicines to help people get healthy.

HELPING HABITATS

Habitats need to have the right amounts of animals and plants to stay healthy. Snakes are predators. They hunt other animals. Eating other animals helps habitats stay balanced.

LIFE CYCLE OF A ROUGH GREEN SNAKE

A life cycle is made up of the stages of change throughout a life. Having young is part of a life cycle. Most snakes have young by laying eggs.

HATCHLING

Snakes break out of their eggs using something called an egg tooth.

EGG

Rough green snakes lay eggs in nests. The eggs are soft and leathery.

GROWTH

Snakes keep growing throughout their lives. This involves <u>shedding</u> their skin.

ADULT

Female snakes lay their own eggs and have their own young.

LIFE CYCLE OF A WATER SNAKE

Some snakes <u>reproduce</u> by giving birth to live young.

EMBRYO

Water snakes grow inside their mother as an <u>embryo</u>. They get all of their food from their mother.

SNAKELET
Water snakes are born in a thin sac.

ADULT
A mother snake does not look after its young once they are born. The young snakes grow into adults. They may have young of their own.

DID YOU KNOW?
Some snakes reproduce by carrying eggs that <u>hatch</u> inside their bodies.

BELIEVE IT OR NOT!

Snakes keep growing throughout their whole lives. The longest known snake was a python. It grew to be nearly 33 feet long!

Snakes need heat from sunlight to stay warm. When the weather get. cold, some snakes hide away to rest. This rest is called brumation.

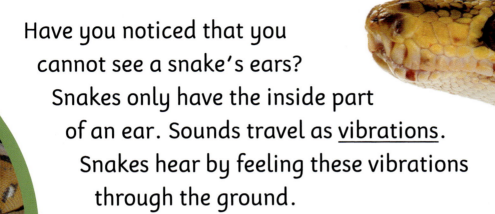

Have you noticed that you cannot see a snake's ears? Snakes only have the inside part of an ear. Sounds travel as <u>vibrations</u>. Snakes hear by feeling these vibrations through the ground.

Some snakes can throw themselves from trees and glide through the air more than 300 feet!

ARE YOU A GENIUS KID?

You are now full of fascinating snake facts that are sure to wow your friends and family. But before you head off to impress your friends, let's test your knowledge. Are you really a genius kid?

Check back through the book if you are not sure.

1. What is special about a snake's tongue?

2. What does cold-blooded mean?

3. What do snake eggs feel like?

Answers:
1. It is forked, which means it is split in two at the end, 2. That an animal's body temperature changes based on their surroundings, 3. Soft and leathery

GLOSSARY

adaptations   changes to animals that have happened over time to help them be better suited to their environment

embryo   an unborn or unhatched animal in the process of development

hatch   when a baby animal comes out of its egg

jaws   the upper and lower parts of the mouth containing the teeth

prey   an animal that is hunted by other animals for food

reproduce   to make more of the same thing; to have young

shedding   when an animal loses a layer of fur or skin to be replaced by another layer from underneath

temperature   how hot or cold something is

venom   a harmful substance that is injected through a bite or sting

vibrations   movements that go up and down, left and right, or back and forward fast

INDEX